The College Essay Builder

"When one has weighed the sun in a balance, and measured the steps of the moon, and mapped out the seven heavens star by star, there still remains oneself."

- Oscar Wilde

Chapters

Introduction..3

Chapter 1: Know Your Objectives..........................5

Chapter 2: Genre, Prompt, Structure....................6

Chapter 3: Literary Devices....................................8

Chapter 4: Writing and Content..........................12

Chapter 5: Common App Prompts......................16

Chapter 6: Coalition Prompts...............................30

Chapter 7: Summary 42

Introduction

Today, many colleges and universities remain test-optional. Consequently, some students and prospective college applicants may not pursue standardized testing for college admission. Nevertheless, the college admission essay, a personal statement, remains essential to many college applications. It is standard for many college application platforms students use to submit their applications.

Ultimately, this book helps applicants better understand how to answer college admission essay prompts, tell their stories, and share their work with institutions that weigh their applications. Those determined to write a winning essay deserve help. Therefore, the following pages introduce students and prospective college applicants to brief, interactive rubrics. Subsequent guidelines assist students in composing successful essays by leveraging several helpful hints and ideas. The aim? To help applicants elevate their writing while making the process less daunting.

The first chapter provides writers with a brief overview of critical objectives while writing. The second chapter introduces writers to the essay's genre, prompt, and structure. Chapter three details several literary devices and techniques writers may use in their narratives. Chapter four offers brief meditations on the "dos and don'ts" of writing a personal narrative for college admission. Finally, this book's fifth and sixth chapters break down sample Common App and Coalition for College essay prompts, followed by the seventh chapter and summary of the book and its contents.

Chapter 1

Know Your Objectives

- [ ] Write a compelling personal statement, story, or narrative.

- [ ] Get your reader to suspend disbelief and discover you through your lived experience.

- [ ] Economize your language:

    - Effectively utilize word counts with literary techniques and devices.

- [ ] Make yourself legible to your reader:

    - If appropriate, use concrete examples to demonstrate that you know the resources, programs, and opportunities available at each college or university when appropriate.

        - Clearly state how you will utilize them and why.

Chapter 2

"Invention, compression, the use of imagination."
— David Lazar, 2008

Genre, Prompt, and Structure

The essay prompts help writers to develop a personal narrative. Both tone and diction help establish the voice of the essay. Writers will also want to use the prompt as a guideline for probing their personal history for material that lets them successfully answer the prompt. A good approach is to understand that, in addition to establishing a useful voice, writers elaborate on their narrative according to a familiar structure: beginning, middle, and end.

The beginning of the personal narrative does more than invite readers to continue; it makes it so that readers want to know more and thus want to continue reading. Opening with dialogue, onomatopoeia, or in the middle of the action are handy ways to establish such a beginning. It also helps establish the tone and voice the reader can expect to continue throughout the rest of the essay.

In the middle section of the essay, writers can "sign-post" or use language from the prompt. This should indicate that the essay effectively answers the prompt, including all aspects. The reader must know that the essay does not just roughly hint at an answer to the prompt but offers substance. Effectively, a successful essay will use the material of the writer's life to answer the prompt and explicitly address the critical aspects the prompt sets out in detail to help guide writers in developing their narrative.

The essay's final section continues incorporating themes and motifs from the first two sections (i.e., beginning and middle). It may include these in new ways or offer a twist. Above all, however, the essay's ending continues the narrative arc, which starts in the beginning part of the essay and carries through the middle into the ending. Reminding readers that the essay has effectively answered the prompt is also important. Ultimately, an effective essay "shows" readers rather than "tells" them what the essay is about.

Chapter 3

Literary Devices, Techniques

Renowned writers and amateurs alike can distinguish themselves through literary devices. Their techniques are one way they demonstrate their skill and capability as writers to their audiences or readers. Prospective college students and applicants writing a personal statement for college admission—the "college essay"—can do the same.

Even having never met the author, readers regularly find promise in continuing to read and hear what the author has to say. If so, they likely perceive value in indulging the author from cover to cover. This is why literary techniques and devices are so important for student writers, too: they can make for a convincing and engaging read.

Reading so many essays is quite an investment. So is the one universities make when selecting students for their admitted pool of applicants or prospective students. Thus, the reward of reading an engaging statement matters.

Device, Definition, Description

Dialogue | In composition, conversation

Dialogue, ex.:

> My dad and I are motoring over the desert floor, cruising 35 miles per hour. Then, our buggy hits a berm we somehow failed to see. I feel the wheels buckle underneath the chassis and hear the shocks snap just before "lift-off." I grab the wheel as tightly as possible; I don't want the imminent rollover to crush my hands. The last thing I tell my dad is, "Brace yourself;" I close my eyes and hope for the best. —Jack P.

Diction | Word choice

Diction, ex.:

> My journey down the beekeeping rabbit hole began during quarantine (during the pandemic and subsequent lockdown). I had started to eat almost all of my food from a small group of raised garden beds that my grandmother and I tended in

Lake Wawasee, Indiana. Likewise, while researching different gardening methods, such as food forests and permaculture, I stumbled upon some beekeeping videos, watched them out of mild interest, and was hooked. I happened to be lucky enough to have a chance to watch videos in which the primary source of instruction was Dr. Leo, who is one of the most experienced and well-researched beekeepers in the United States; as such, I was exposed to many different styles of beekeeping apart from the standard American one. Ultimately, I started to keep bees of my own. —JR L.

Imagery | Using the five senses

Imagery, ex.:

I woke up at 5:30 a.m., unaware of what the day had in store. Shortly after, I entered a brightly lit warehouse and immediately noticed the oppressive heat and moisture trapped inside by the broiling Arizona summer. The fans inside blew hot air onto my face like oversized hairdryers, making me sweat even more profusely. —Mason W.

In media res | In the middle of the action

In media res, ex.:

> The goalie from the opposing team punted the ball down the pitch. Their striker and I rocketed into the cold winter air to make the header. My head bounced off hers like a frozen grapefruit. Then, suddenly, I was on the floor, dazed. —Mackenzie C.

Onomatopoeia | Something named for how it sounds

Onomatopoeia, ex.:

> *Whap!*
>
> My friend's resistance band snapping loose is the last thing I hear before it strikes me in the eye, and I collapse to the floor. Hours later, I awake with the only vision I have left in one eye and multiple side effects from blindness in the other. —Perla A.

Chapter 4

Your writing and its contents...

1. Make the read enjoyable.

    When developing writing, utilize specific literary techniques and devices from the outset and weave themes and motifs throughout the college essay.

2. Who are you?

    Applicants are unique individuals with distinctive voices. Literary devices and an adequate command of prose help writers develop apt expressions of themselves so the reader can get to know them better. Deliberate stories can help establish a connection between reader and author, making the essay not only a personal statement but a memorable one.

3. Creativity is a good thing but not everything.

    Themes and motifs may present themselves organically in your writing. Take advantage, but be measured. Using techniques and devices in writing serves the statement, not vice versa. Applying creative techniques shows creativity, critical thinking, and command of good writing skills.

4. Writing skills can be shorthand for intelligence, effort, and promise.

   Some ideas are complex, which can make them challenging to pen. Literary devices help alleviate some of the burden of effectively communicating them. Concision and diction, or word choice, help students develop a narrative that reflects growth, perseverance, and wisdom without risking critical elements getting lost in a sea of words.

5. How deep does the rabbit hole go?

   Showcasing one's depth as a thinker and a human being can be highly relevant to one's narrative. However, writers will likely have to make selective choices about which points to emphasize. The prompt and word count can inform and assist with such decisions.

6. Don't sell yourself short: you have a genuine story.

There is much to convey, and establishing credibility with one's reader matters. Share your human experience. Experience can mean one has the authority to speak on a particular topic, but this authority has reasonable limits: every perspective is partial and subjective. Students can craft a compelling narrative and memorable personal statement by writing logically, coherently, and incorporating emotion.

7. Make a lasting impression.

   Personal statements like the college admission essay can be memorable for several reasons. Again, the prompt itself is instrumental in guiding the essay's focus. Poignancy or creativity does not solely guarantee that an essay succeeds in being memorable while aptly addressing the prompt.

8. Illustrating Themes and Values

   The college essay can reveal much about an applicant's beliefs or values. Literary techniques and devices can help the writer share these genuinely to create a deep understanding.

9. You can relate...

> Feel free to use a first-person perspective when writing your statement.

10. Be uniquely yourself.

> A quality essay can help students stick out among a pool of similarly qualified applicants. One way to write a winning personal statement is to select a prompt that makes space for one's story while allowing one to showcase a skillful use of literary techniques and devices.

Chapter 5

Sample Common App Essay Prompts

1. "Some students have a background, identity, interest, or talent that is so meaningful they believe their application would be incomplete without it. If this sounds like you, then please share your story."

The first essay prompt on the Common App platform allows writers to say more about themselves. Indeed, there is likely much more to students than grades, standardized test scores, letters of recommendation, or extracurricular activities alone. Writers may use the personal narrative genre and literary techniques and devices explored above to address this prompt.

Builder:

What aspect of the prompt will your essay address?

- ☐ Background
- ☐ Identity
- ☐ Interest
- ☐ Talent
- ☐ Other

Why is this aspect meaningful to you?

What makes it more meaningful than the others?

Why would your application be "incomplete" without it?

What is your story?

How does your background, identity, interest, or talent fit your story?

2. "The lessons we take from obstacles we encounter can be fundamental to later success. Recount a time when you faced a challenge, setback, or failure. How did it affect you, and what did you learn from the experience?"

Ad astra per aspera. In English: through adversity, the stars. Here, writers may discuss their experience with adversity, including how it translated into something positive in their lives. This prompt, among other possibilities, allows writers to convey a unique aspect of their character: what happens when things do not go according to plan or simply deteriorate altogether. Furthermore, what positive results from the experience were there?

Builder:

What did you face?

What did you come up against?

- ☐ Challenge
- ☐ Setback
- ☐ Failure

In what way(s) did this affect you?

Did you learn something from it? If so, what?

Did you get something out of the experience? If so, then...

Did it eventually make you "successful" in some way? How?

3. "Reflect on a time when you questioned or challenged a belief or idea. What prompted your thinking? What was the outcome?"

Some writers are problem-solvers and may have experience confronting the status quo in their own way. Here is an opportunity for such writers to speak their piece and describe the situation, actions, and results. Hopefully, the story told says something meaningful about the writers themselves in the process.

Builder:

Is it a belief or an idea?

☐ Belief
☐ Idea

What is it, exactly?

What caused you to think about this?

What brought it up for you?

What happened, ultimately?

What was the result?

4. "Reflect on something that someone has done for you that has made you happy or thankful in a surprising way. How has this gratitude affected or motivated you?"

Gratitude is powerful. Writers often receive something or some action that has given them cause to be grateful. Sharing this information with readers places them in the writer's shoes, allowing a unique perspective on the situation, details, and outcomes.

Builder:

Has anyone ever done something for you? If so, how did it make you feel?

- ☐ Happy
- ☐ Thankful (think *grateful*)

What made it so surprising?

How did it surprise you?

How did it affect you?

How did it make you feel?

Why? Did it motivate you? If so, how?

5. "Discuss an accomplishment, event, or realization that sparked a period of personal growth and a new understanding of yourself or others."

Reflecting on some aspect of a writer's life can reveal growth. This includes the catalyst for that growth and how the writer responded to it. The result may also include a new perspective, whether about the writers themselves or others.

Builder:

Identify something that made you grow and understand yourself (or others) differently.

What is it?

- ☐ Accomplishment
- ☐ Event
- ☐ Realization

If you selected one of these, then why?

What made you pick it over the others?

Did it make you understand yourself/others in a new way?

Why did it make you see yourself/others this way?

6. "Describe a topic, idea, or concept you find so engaging that it makes you lose [track] of time. Why does it captivate you? What or who do you turn to when you want to learn more?"

Some writers have many passions, including one that may stick out above the rest. For some, this passion may incur a great investment in terms of time. Something so important in a writer's life can say much about who the writer is, and what unique talents and interests they may bring with them to their future college community.

Builder:

Describe what you love spending time doing. What is it?

Is it a topic, an idea, or a concept, specifically? If so, you can pick one.

- ☐ Topic
- ☐ Idea
- ☐ Concept

Why do you enjoy doing it?

Why is it more enjoyable than everything else?

When you want to know more, what do you do?

How do you learn more about it?

7. "Share an essay on any topic of your choice. It can be one you've already written, one that responds to a different prompt, or one of your own design."

Some writers may have writing of their own that they wish to submit in lieu of writing to one of the above prompts. This can be a creative space for writers whose sense of direction they wish to take is unique but still informs readers personally and compellingly.

Builder:

Be careful: There is freedom in writing to this prompt over the others.

If this is your prompt of choice, ask yourself:

- ☐ Is my submission an edited work that a teacher or tutor assisted me in crafting?
- ☐ Is there a piece you turned in for a grade that you can now truncate to meet the word limit imposed by the Common App essay portion of your college application?

If the answer to any of the questions above was affirmative, consider the works that came to mind as a starting point.

Chapter 6

Sample <u>Coalition for College</u> Essay Prompts

1. "Tell a story from your life, describing an experience that either demonstrates your character or helped to shape it."

Readers will want to know more about the writer so they can get to know the writer beyond the other dimensions and metrics of their application. Here is a prompt allowing writers to share who they are by digging into their experiences. Everyone has a unique story, so letting the reader share in one's human experience is vital.

Builder:

What aspect of the prompt (i.e., a story from your life) will your essay address?

- ☐ An experience that demonstrates your character
- ☐ An experience that helped shape your character
- ☐ Other:

What is the experience? Describe it.

How does it demonstrate your character?

Or, how did it help shape who you are?

2. "What interests or excites you? How does it shape who you are now or who you might become in the future?"

See the accompanying notes on essay prompt number 6 from the Common App essay questions section above.

Builder:

What aspect of the prompt (i.e., an interest) will your essay address?

- ☐ An interest
- ☐ Something else in life that excites you
- ☐ Other

What is this thing that excites you? Describe it.

How does it shape you right now?

How will it shape you, or who you are, going forward?

3. "Describe a time when you had a positive impact on others. What were the challenges? What were the rewards?"

Writers might wish to express a time when they have positively impacted their community or one of its members. This information can help illuminate their character for readers.

Builder:

When did you positively impact someone else or a group?

Describe the challenges you faced.

What action(s) did you take?

How did you benefit from it?

What were some of the positive outcomes?

4. "Has there been a time when an idea or belief of yours was questioned? How did you respond? What did you learn?"

See the accompanying notes on essay prompt number 3 from the Common App essay questions section above.

Builder:

Which will you discuss in your essay?

- ☐ A belief
- ☐ An idea
- ☐ Other:

When did you have, or face, this experience?

How did it come about?

Was it planned or accidental?

What was your response?

How did you react?

What did you take away from the experience?

What lesson(s) did it teach you?

5. "What success have you achieved or obstacle have you faced? What advice would you give a sibling or friend going through a similar experience?"

See the accompanying notes on essay prompt number 2 from the Common App essay questions section above.

Builder:

Which will you discuss in your essay?

- ☐ The success you achieved
- ☐ An obstacle you faced
- ☐ Other:

What would you share if someone were to go through a similar experience?

What should they know or be aware of based on your own experience?

6. "Submit an essay on a topic of your choice."

See the accompanying notes on essay prompt number 7 from the Common App essay questions section above.

Builder:

Be careful: There is a unique degree of freedom in writing to this prompt over the others.

If this is your prompt of choice, ask yourself:

- ☐ Is my submission an edited work that a teacher or tutor assisted me in crafting?

- ☐ Is there a piece you turned in for a grade that you can now truncate to meet the word limit imposed by the Common App essay portion of your college application?

As with *Common App* (i.e., sample essay question 7 above), if the answer to any of the previous questions was affirmative, it may be helpful to consider whatever completed written works came to mind. These may be good points from which to begin.

Chapter 7

Summary

A brief review of this book

The first chapter provides writers with a brief overview of critical objectives while writing.

The second chapter introduces writers to the essay's genre, prompt, and structure.

Chapter three details several literary devices and techniques writers may use in their narratives.

Chapter four offers brief meditations on the "dos and don'ts" of writing a personal narrative for college admission.

Finally, this book's fifth and sixth chapters summarize sample Common App and Coalition for College essay prompts.

Made in the USA
Columbia, SC
27 August 2024